Where Is Everybody?

Where Is Everybody?

AN ANIMAL ALPHABET BY
Eve Merriam

WITH ILLUSTRATIONS BY
Diane de Groat

SIMON AND SCHUSTER BOOKS FOR YOUNG READERS
Published by Simon & Schuster Inc., New York

To my two favorite photographers in the world,
Ellen and Pam

—Eve Merriam

For my niece, Julie Soller,
because she knows a vicuna when she sees one

—Diane de Groat

SIMON AND SCHUSTER BOOKS FOR YOUNG READERS
Simon & Schuster Building, Rockefeller Center,
1230 Avenue of the Americas, New York, New York 10020.
Text copyright © 1989 by Eve Merriam
Illustrations copyright © 1989 by Diane de Groat
SIMON AND SCHUSTER BOOKS FOR YOUNG READERS
is a trademark of Simon & Schuster Inc.
Designed by Mary Ahern
Manufactured in the United States of America

10 9 8 7 6 5 4 3 2 1

Library of Congress Cataloging-in-Publication Data
Merriam, Eve.
Where is everybody? : an animal alphabet.
SUMMARY: A humorous alphabet of animals engaged in human
activities, including an alligator in the attic, a unicorn
underwater, and an elephant riding on the escalator.
1. English language—Alphabet—Juvenile literature.   2. Animals-
-Juvenile literature.   [1. Alphabet. 2. Animals.] I. De Groat, Diane, ill.
II. Title.   PE1155.M48   1989   ISBN 0-671-64964-7   88-19800

Alligator is in the attic.

Bear is in the bakery.

C at is at the computer.

Dog is at the daycare center.

E lephant is on the escalator.

F rog is in the factory.

Giraffe is in the garage.

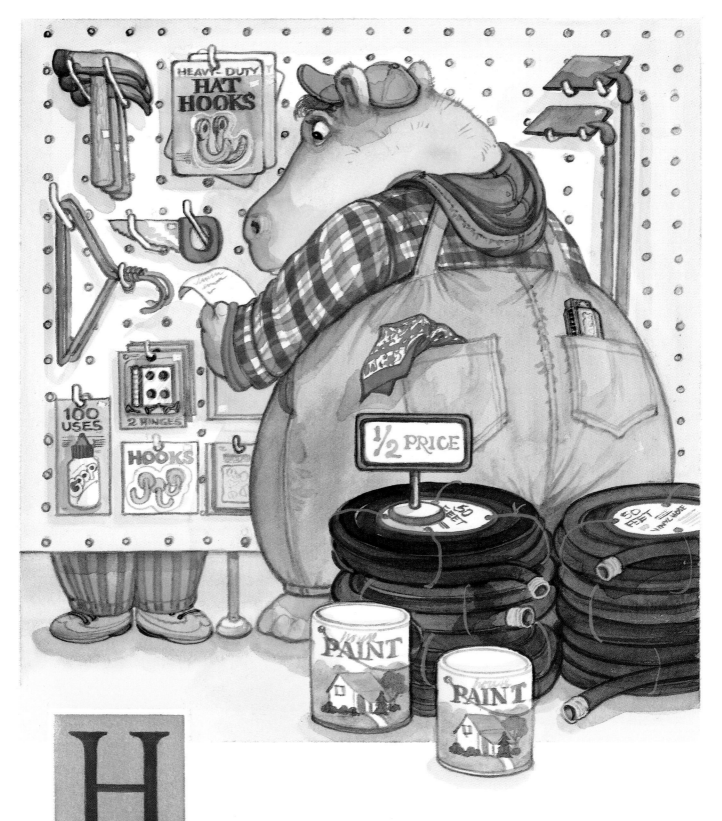

H

ippopotamus is in the hardware store.

I bex is on the ice.

J aguar is on the jungle gym.

K angaroo is in the kitchen.

Lion is in the laundry room.

Monkey is in the market.

arwhal is in the noodle house.

O wl is in the opera.

P enguin is in the Post Office.

 uail is on the quarterdeck.

R abbit is on the roller coaster.

 heep is in the stroller.

Tiger is in the taxi.

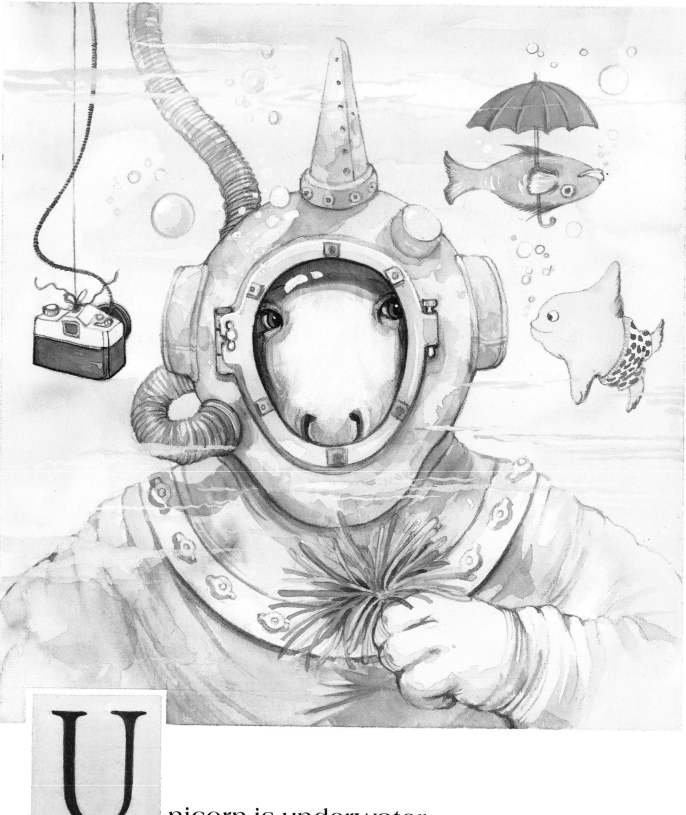

U

nicorn is underwater.

V icuna is at the video store.

Walrus is at the wheel.

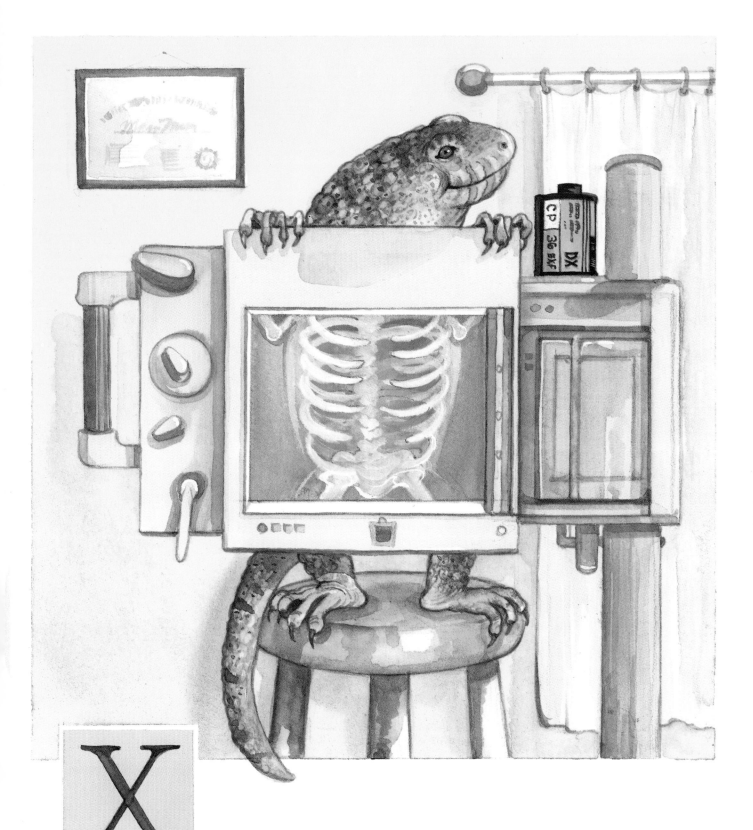

X enosaurid is at the X-ray machine.

Yak is in the yard.

Zebra is at the zoo.